TOP 30
S Q L
INTERVIEW
CODING TASKS
WITH WINNING SOLUTIONS

TOP 30 SQL Interview Coding Tasks with Winning Solutions
by Matthew Urban

August 2018: First Edition

Proofreader: Alex Solsbery
Illustrator: Matthew Urban
Cover designer: Karolina Kaiser
Composition: Karolina Kaiser (mobisfera.pl)

ISBN 978-83-65477-14-9

Preface

SQL is one of the most common programming languages used to manipulate data. If you are a developer, there is a 99% probability that during a job interview you will be asked to solve a couple of coding tasks from SQL. If you are a recruiter, this book gives you a ready to use set of coding tasks with correct answers.

Matthew Urban
IT specialist, Senior Java developer

Data-set

From the perspective of a recruiter, it is easier to use the same data-set during each job interview as is the case with this book. For simplicity, the database schema of a small e-commerce system is used. It contains the following tables: customers, products, suppliers, orders and order_items. Each coding task described in this book is based on the data-set given below.

Table 1.1 – Example data-set of customers table.

customers

ID	FIRST_NAME	LAST_NAME	EMAIL	PHONE	COUNTRY
1	Boris	Spassky	boris@spassky.com	999-888-123	Russia
2	Akiba	Rubinstein	rubi@chess.com	NULL	Poland
3	Bobby	Fischer	bobby@fishcher.com	210-6221-9101-22	USA
4	Jose	Capabalnca	play@capablanca.com	032-345-567-678	Cuba

Table 1.2 – Example data-set of products table.

products

ID	NAME	AVAILABLE	PRICE	SUPPLIER
1	Baby diaper	true	12	Brandon
2	Crossland bike	true	780	X-Bikes
3	Bicycle helmet	true	50	X-Bikes
4	Energy drink	false	5	Nutrition-V
5	LED bulb	true	30	Electronics Master

Table 1.3 – Example data-set of `suppliers` table.

suppliers

ID	COMPANY_NAME	CONTACT_NAME	ADDRESS	COUNTRY	EMAIL
1	X-Bikes	Malcom Xavery	New York, Yellow 12	USA	malcolm@xbikes.com
2	Brandon	Veronica Brandon	Chicago, Barbecue 780/2	USA	veronica@brandon.com

Table 1.4 – Example data-set of `orders` table.

orders

ID	ORDER_DATE	SHIPPED_DATE	CUSTOMER_ID
1	2014-11-25	2014-12-02	3
2	2016-12-02	2016-12-09	3
3	2017-02-10	2017-02-18	1
4	2018-03-10	2018-03-19	4
5	2019-09-20	2019-09-30	4

Table 1.5 – Example data-set of `order_items` table.

order_items

ORDER_ID	PRODUCT_ID	QUANTITY	PRICE	DISCOUNT
1	2	1	780	0
1	3	1	50	0
2	3	2	50	50
3	5	1	30	30

1. Get data from the database.

The easiest way to verify if a person knows the basics of SQL is to ask them to retrieve data from a database.

Solution

Given three tables: `customers`, `products` and `orders` you need to create queries which retrieve all rows from them. Listing 1.1 presents simple `SELECT` statements.

Listing 1.1 – Example of simple `SELECT` statements.

```
SELECT * FROM customers;

SELECT * FROM products;

SELECT * FROM orders;
```

Please notice that the wildcard (*) causes all columns to be retrieved. In many cases, it is necessary to retrieve only part of the data. Listing 1.2 presents an example `SELECT` statement which retrieves only the first and last name of a customer.

Listing 1.2 – The `SELECT` statement which gets specified columns.

```
SELECT first_name, last_name FROM customers;
```

2. Get data from the database using a conditional statement.

Preparing conditional statements is one of the necessary skills every programmer must have. A developer needs to create queries which return only those records that fulfill a specified condition. To retrieve filtered data, the WHERE clause combined with AND, OR and NOT operators should be used.

WHERE

First, you are asked to prepare a query which returns all customers which are from the USA.

Listing 2.1 – Example of SELECT statement with WHERE clause.

```sql
SELECT * FROM customers
  WHERE country = 'USA';
```

OR

Second, you are asked to prepare a query which returns all customers which are from the USA or Canada.

Listing 2.2 – Example of SELECT statement with OR operator.

```sql
SELECT * FROM customers
  WHERE country = 'USA' OR country = 'Canada';
```

AND

Finally, the last most basic operator. You need to prepare a query which returns all products from supplier 'Brandon' and price lower than $20.

Listing 2.3 – Example of SELECT statement with AND operator.

```sql
SELECT * FROM products
  WHERE supplier = 'Brandon' AND price < 20;
```

3. Get data from the database using the IN operator.

The IN operator is very often used in SELECT statements. The IN operator can be seen as shorthand for multiple OR conditions, but it can also take the results from other SELECT queries as input.

List of values

You are asked to prepare a query which returns all customers which are from the following list of countries:

- USA,
- Canada,
- Australia,
- Great Britain,
- New Zealand.

Listing 3.1 presents the correct implementation of such a query.

Listing 3.1 – Example of SELECT statement with IN operator.

```
SELECT * FROM customers
  WHERE country IN ('USA', 'Canada', 'Australia' , 'Great Britain',
'New Zealand');
```

Subquery

Another way to use the IN clause is to pass a list of values by selecting data from another table. For example, you may be asked to retrieve products which were sold in quantities higher than 100. Listing 3.2 presents an example of such a query. From the order_items table, you retrieve a list of products identifiers which sold more than 100 items in one order. Next, such a list is passed to the IN clause. Finally, the SELECT statement returns all products which match previously selected identifiers.

Listing 3.2 – Example of subquery.

```sql
SELECT * FROM products
  WHERE id IN (SELECT product_id FROM order_items
                  WHERE quantity > 100);
```

4. Save data in the database.

A list of most basic data operations contains save, update, delete and read. Each developer needs to be aware of how to save data in the database before he can modify, delete or read it. To put new rows into an existing table, the SQL provides the `INSERT INTO` statement.

INSERT INTO

In most cases during a job interview, you are asked to save a new customer and a new product in the database. Listing 4.1 presents a correct solution.

Listing 4.1 – Examples of `INSERT INTO` statement.

```sql
INSERT INTO customers (first_name, last_name, email, phone, country)
   VALUES ('John', 'Malkovich', 'malkovich@yahoo.com', NULL, 'Mexico');

INSERT INTO products (name, available, price, supplier)
   VALUES ('Bike', true, 465, 'T&D');
```

5. Modify data in the database.

The UPDATE statement is used to modify existing records in the database. The syntax of UPDATE allows you to modify selected columns in one or more rows at once. If you do not specify the WHERE clause, all records are going to be updated.

UPDATE

You are usually asked to prepare three UPDATE queries: one which modifies all records, a second which modifies only a single record and a third which modifies a subset of data. For example, you need to write a query which removes all phone numbers of all customers. Listing 5.1 presents a solution.

Listing 5.1 – Example of UPDATE statement which modifies all rows.

```
UPDATE customers
   SET phone = NULL;
```

Next, you need to prepare a query which modifies the name of a product with identifier 6, as presented in Listing 5.2.

Listing 5.2 – Example of UPDATE statement which modifies a single row.

```
UPDATE products
   SET name = 'Crossland bike'
   WHERE id = 6;
```

Finally, you are asked to prepare a query which modifies the shipping date of all orders placed on 2018-09-15.

Listing 5.3 – Example of UPDATE statement which modifies multiple rows.

```
UPDATE orders
   SET shipping_date = 2018-10-01
   WHERE order_date = 2018-09-15;
```

6. Remove data from the database.

Managing enormous amounts of data has become standard today. In many systems, outdated data is transferred to another repository, and removed from the database. Every developer needs to be aware of how to use the DELETE statement and remove existing records from the table.

DELETE

In most cases, during a job interview, you will be asked to delete a customer or a product from the database.

Listing 6.1 – Examples of DELETE statement.

```sql
DELETE FROM customers WHERE id = 10;

DELETE FROM products WHERE id = 6;
```

Recruiters like to ask what will happen if you forget the WHERE clause. The correct answer is: all records will be deleted. An example of such a query is presented in Listing 6.2.

Listing 6.2 – Remove all records from table.

```sql
DELETE FROM orders;
```

7. Find rows which values are NULL.

The most commonly used coding task which verifies if a developer knows the basics of SQL is to write a query which selects data by the NULL column value. Please note that NULL value is not the same thing as an empty text value or zero number. In simple terms, NULL means there is no value.

IS NULL

You are asked to create a query which returns all products without a name. The trick here is that you can easily create an incorrect query. Listing 7.1 presents a correct and incorrect implementation of such a query.

Listing 7.1 – Example of IS NULL operator usage.

```
--INCORRECT
SELECT * FROM products
   WHERE name = NULL;

--CORRECT
SELECT * FROM products
   WHERE name IS NULL;
```

IS NOT NULL

It is also incorrect to test if any value in a given column is not NULL by using the != operator. Listing 7.2 presents an incorrect and correct implementation of a query which gets products which name is not NULL.

Listing 7.2 – Example of IS NOT NULL operator usage.

```
--INCORRECT
SELECT * FROM products
   WHERE name != NULL;

--CORRECT
SELECT * FROM products
   WHERE name IS NOT NULL;
```

8. Get list of unique values from table column.

In some scenarios, you are interested only in unique values, or in other words, you want to omit duplicate values in the result set. The `SELECT DISTINCT` statement should be used to return unique values.

DISTINCT

During a job interview, you are asked to retrieve a unique list of countries based on the `customers` table and the `country` column. Listing 8.1 presents an example query which returns a list of unique values from a table column.

Listing 8.1 – Example of `SELECT DISTINCT` statement usage.

```
SELECT DISTINCT country FROM customers;
```

As a result, such a query returns a list of countries without duplicates.

9. Sort results.

Sorting is one of the most commonly used features within the SELECT query. Every developer needs to be aware that the ORDER BY keyword is used to sort the result-set.

ORDER BY

One of the most frequently asked SQL question during every job interview is to sort customers by name. Please notice that the ORDER BY clause allows you to sort results in ascending or descending order, using a single or several columns. Listing 9.1 presents SELECT queries which sort customers by the first name and last name in different ways.

Listing 9.1 – Examples of ORDER BY clause usage.

```sql
SELECT * FROM customers ORDER BY first_name;

SELECT * FROM customers ORDER BY last_name;

SELECT * FROM customers ORDER BY last_name ASC, first_name DESC;
```

10. Get results based on text pattern.

A database engine can be used as a simple text search engine. Remember that for complex search text queries, the database engine is not enough. The database can be used to fulfill only the simple requirements.

LIKE

The `LIKE` operator used within the `WHERE` clause permits to define a text pattern, which is used by the database engine. The engine matches every value of a given column with the pattern. If the text value matches a pattern, a record is returned. A pattern may contain only two wildcards: `_` (underscore line) and `%` (percent). The underscore line represents any single character, while percent: zero, one, or more of any characters. During the job interview, you are usually asked to return all customers whose first name starts with the letter A, or products which contain the phrase 'bike' inside.

Listing 10.1 – Example of `LIKE` operator usage.

```sql
SELECT * FROM customers
  WHERE first_name LIKE 'A%';

SELECT * FROM products
  WHERE name LIKE '%bike%';
```

11. Create and use an index.

Understanding data structures used inside a database is crucial for every developer. An index is an additional data structure (usually a b-tree) used to speed up data retrieval queries. Every recruiter needs to check if a developer is familiar with basic concepts behind the database index.

CREATE INDEX

Let us assume that customers are identified in an external system by email field, and there is a need to create a service which returns the customer connected with the particular email address. You are asked to create and use an index. Listing 11.1 presents how to create an index on the `email` column.

Listing 11.1 – Example of `CREATE INDEX` statement.

```
CREATE INDEX idx_customer_email ON customers (email);
```

The query presented in Listing 11.2 performs a full table scan to find a customer without a proper index. After the index is created, you don't have to change the query to make it efficient. Under the hood, the database engine takes advantage of a b-tree data structure and performs just a couple of steps to find the customer you are looking for.

Listing 11.2 – Example of `SELECT` statement which uses an index.

```
SELECT * FROM customers WHERE email = 'bobby@fisher.com';
```

12. Create and use composite index.

Indexes are used to speed-up search queries execution. The index may include a single column or multiple columns. An index which includes more than one column is known as a composite index.

Composite index

A composite index is very similar to a phone book. In a phone book, persons are first sorted by the last name and then by the first name. As a result of such sorting, you first search for a phone number of a person by the last name, and then by the first name. It is impossible to find a person by only the first name effectively. The most important conclusion is that the order of columns in a composite index is crucial for performance.

CREATE INDEX

During a job interview, you are asked to create a composite index on the order_items table using two columns: order_id and product_id. Listing 12.1 presents how to create a composite index.

Listing 12.1 – Example of composite index definition.

```
CREATE INDEX idx_order_product_id ON order_items (order_id, product_id);
```

After that, a recruiter presents four SELECT statements and asks which ones use the idx_order_product_id index and why? Listing 12.2 presents such SELECT queries.

Listing 12.2 – Example usage of composite index.

```
-- 1
SELECT * FROM order_items WHERE order_id = 3;

-- 2
SELECT * FROM order_items WHERE product_id = 2;

-- 3
SELECT * FROM order_items WHERE order_id = 3 AND product_id = 2;
```

```
-- 4
SELECT * FROM order_items WHERE product_id = 2 AND order_id = 3;
```

Keeping in mind how to find entries in a phone book it is easy to provide a correct answer. Because the `order_id` column is defined as first in the composite index, the first `SELECT` statement uses the index. Because the `product_id` column is defined as second in the composite index, the second `SELECT` statement does not use the index. Finally, the composite index is used by both: a third and fourth `SELECT` statement. In the same way, as you search for a person in the phone book by the last name and then by the first name, the database engine first searches by `order_id` column and then by `product_id` column. The order of conditions inside the `WHERE` clause does not matter because the `AND` operator is symmetric.

13. Prepare inner, left outer, right outer, and full outer table joins.

Assuming that a developer does not have to create joins to retrieve data is incorrect. Almost every system retrieves related data from many tables in a single query. For example, to read customers and their orders a developer needs to join two tables: customers with orders. Usually, during a job interview process, a developer needs to create four most commonly used types of joins:

- INNER JOIN,
- LEFT OUTER JOIN,
- RIGHT OUTER JOIN,
- FULL OUTER JOIN.

Please also note that the data-set prepared for this task highlights the differences between different types of joins:

- Some orders have existing customers assigned.
- Some orders have non-existing customers assigned.
- Some customers did not make any order yet.

INNER JOIN

You are asked to create an INNER JOIN between customers and orders tables. Listing 13.1 presents an example SELECT statement which joins two tables using the INNER JOIN keyword. Next, you are asked by a recruiter about the result. The correct answer is: the inner join matches rows that exist, and excludes all non-matching rows.

Listing 13.1 – Example of INNER JOIN keyword usage.

```
SELECT c.*, o.* FROM customers c
  INNER JOIN orders o ON c.id = o.customer_id;
```

Figure 13.1 presents a visual explanation of INNER JOIN by a Venn diagram.

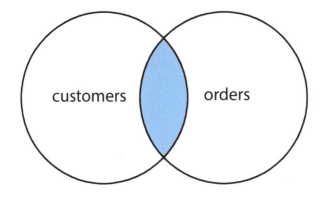

```
SELECT c.*, o.* FROM customers c
   INNER JOIN orders o ON c.id = o.customer_id;
```

C.FIRST_NAME	C.LAST_NAME	C.ID	O.CUSTOMER_ID	O.ORDER_DATE	O.ID
Bobby	Fischer	3	3	2014-11-25	1
Bobby	Fischer	3	3	2016-12-02	2
Boris	Spassky	1	1	2018-03-10	4
Jose	Capablanca	4	4	2019-09-20	5

Figure 13.1 – The INNER JOIN represented as an intersection of sets.

LEFT OUTER JOIN

In case of the LEFT OUTER JOIN, you need to know that such a join returns all rows from the left table with matching rows from the right table. But if there is no match, values of the right table are null. Listing 13.2 presents an example SELECT statement which joins two tables using the LEFT OUTER JOIN keyword.

Listing 13.2 – Example of LEFT OUTER JOIN keyword usage.

```
SELECT c.*, o.* FROM customers c
   LEFT OUTER JOIN orders o ON c.id = o.customer_id;
```

Figure 13.2 presents a visual explanation of LEFT OUTER JOIN by a Venn diagram.

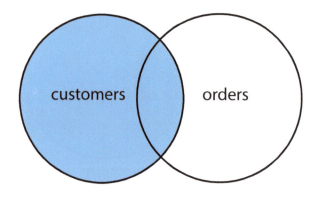

```
SELECT c.*, o.* FROM customers c
    LEFT OUTER JOIN orders o ON c.id = o.customer_id;
```

C.FIRST_NAME	C.LAST_NAME	C.ID	O.CUSTOMER_ID	O.ORDER_DATE	O.ID
Boris	Spassky	1	1	2018-03-19	4
Akiba	Rubinstein	2	NULL	NULL	NULL
Bobby	Fischer	3	3	2014-12-02	1
Bobby	Fischer	3	3	2016-12-09	2
Jose	Capablanca	4	4	2019-09-20	5

Figure 13.2 – The LEFT OUTER JOIN represented as an intersection of sets.

RIGHT OUTER JOIN

If you are familiar with the LEFT OUTER JOIN, for formalities, you might be asked about the RIGHT OUTER JOIN. The correct answer is: the right outer join returns all rows from the right table with matching rows from the left table. But if there is no match, values of the left table are null. Listing 13.3 presents an example SELECT statement which joins two tables using the RIGHT OUTER JOIN keyword.

Listing 13.3 – Example of `RIGHT OUTER JOIN` keyword usage.

```sql
SELECT c.*, o.* FROM customers c
  RIGHT OUTER JOIN orders o ON c.id = o.customer_id;
```

Figure 13.3 presents a visual explanation of `RIGHT OUTER JOIN` by a Venn diagram.

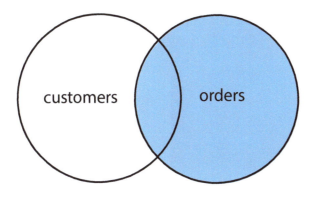

```sql
SELECT c.*, o.* FROM customers c
  RIGHT OUTER JOIN orders o ON c.id = o.customer_id;
```

C.FIRST_NAME	C.LAST_NAME	C.ID	O.CUSTOMER_ID	O.ORDER_DATE	O.ID
Bobby	Fischer	3	3	2014-11-25	1
Bobby	Fischer	3	3	2016-12-02	2
NULL	NULL	NULL	10	2017-02-10	3
Boris	Spassky	1	1	2018-03-10	4
Jose	Capablanca	4	4	2019-09-20	5

Figure 13.3 – The `RIGHT OUTER JOIN` represented as an intersection of sets.

FULL OUTER JOIN

Finally, you are asked to create a `FULL OUTER JOIN` between `customers` and `orders` tables. Listing 13.4 presents an example `SELECT` statement which joins two tables using the `FULL OUTER JOIN` keyword. You also need to know that the full outer join matches rows that exist, and includes all non-matching rows from both, the left and right table. If there is no match, the `null` values are returned.

Listing 13.4 – Example of FULL OUTER JOIN keyword usage.

```sql
SELECT c.*, o.* FROM customers c
  FULL OUTER JOIN orders o ON c.id = o.customer_id;
```

Figure 13.4 presents a visual explanation of FULL OUTER JOIN by a Venn diagram.

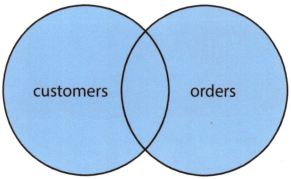

```sql
SELECT c.* , o.* FROM customers c
  FULL OUTER JOIN orders o ON c.id = o.customer_id;
```

C.FIRST_NAME	C.LAST_NAME	C.ID	O.CUSTOMER_ID	O.ORDER_DATE	O.ID
Boris	Spassky	1	1	2018-03-19	4
Akiba	Rubinstein	2	NULL	NULL	NULL
Bobby	Fischer	3	3	2014-12-02	1
Bobby	Fischer	3	3	2016-12-09	2
Jose	Capablanca	4	4	2019-09-20	5
NULL	NULL	NULL	10	2017-02-10	3

Figure 13.4 – The FULL OUTER JOIN represented as an intersection of sets.

14. Download aggregated data from the database.

Many queries need to perform aggregate operations. Aggregate operations are used by a developer to return the number of rows, the minimum, average, maximum value, or summed values of numeric columns in a given data set.

COUNT()

You are usually asked to count the number of customers in the given database. Listing 14.1 presents an example of such a query.

Listing 14.1 – Example of COUNT() aggregate function usage.

```
SELECT COUNT(*) FROM customers;
```

AVG()

Another very popular SQL interview task is to calculate the average price of a product in a given database. Listing 14.2 presents a correct solution.

Listing 14.2 – Example of AVG() aggregate function usage.

```
SELECT AVG(price) FROM products;
```

MIN() & MAX()

In the same manner as the average price, you are asked to find out the minimum and maximum price of products.

Listing 14.3 – Example of MIN() and MAX() aggregate functions usage.

```
SELECT MIN(price) FROM products;

SELECT MAX(price) FROM products;
```

SUM()

The last task to verify the basic usage of aggregate functions is, to sum the quantity of all products in the specified order. Listing 14.4 presents a query which returns a summary quantity of all products delivered with order identifier 28.

Listing 14.4 – Example of SUM() aggregate function usage.

```
SELECT SUM(quantity) FROM order_items WHERE order_id = 28;
```

15. Download aggregated results grouped by column.

Specific columns can be used to group the results of queries which use aggregate functions. Moreover, a developer can restrict such a result set by specifying a condition.

GROUP BY

You are usually asked to prepare a query which counts a number of products from the same supplier. A query which solves this task should use GROUP BY statement as presented in Listing 15.1. The database groups results of aggregate function by supplier column, which means you get a report of how many products you have from each supplier.

Listing 15.1 – Example of GROUP BY statement usage.

```
SELECT supplier, COUNT(supplier) FROM products GROUP BY supplier;
```

HAVING

Another extension of such a query is to add a conditional statement by using the HAVING clause. During the interview, you are asked to write a query which returns suppliers with less than ten products. Listing 15.2 presents a query which fills these criteria.

Listing 15.2 – Example of HAVING clause usage.

```
SELECT supplier, COUNT(supplier) FROM products
  GROUP BY supplier HAVING COUNT(supplier) < 10;
```

Another commonly asked SQL task is to return first names of customers which occur more than once. To solve this task, you need to create a query with GROUP BY and HAVING keywords as presented in Listing 15.3.

Listing 15.3 – Another example of HAVING clause usage.

```
SELECT first_name, COUNT(first_name) FROM customers
  GROUP BY first_name HAVING COUNT(first_name) > 1;
```

16. Use a function in SQL query.

SQL became a standard of the ANSI (American National Standards Institute) in 1986, and of the ISO (International Organization for Standardization) in 1987. Each database vendor follows the standard, while under the hood operations may be implemented differently by them. However, the SQL standard lacks ready to use functions, and almost every database vendor has a different set of functions. During the job interview the developer does not have to be familiar with the API of a specific vendor, but he must know how to use its functions.

LOWER()

Given a function LOWER(), which converts all uppercase characters to lower case, you need to create a query which returns all customers of which the first name is Mike, MIKE, mike, MiKe, etc. In other words, a text value of first_name column in lower case must match the value mike.

Listing 16.1 – Example of LOWER() function usage.

```sql
SELECT * FROM customers
   WHERE LOWER(first_name) = 'mike';
```

CONCAT()

Given a function CONCAT(), which concatenates multiple character expressions together, you need to create a query which returns a name column as a concatenation of first_name, the space character and last_name.

Listing 16.2 – Example of CONCAT() function usage.

```sql
SELECT CONCAT(first_name, ' ', last_name) AS name
   FROM customers;
```

REPLACE()

Given a function `REPLACE()`, which replaces all occurrences of a specified text, you need to create a query which replaces all – characters with empty text in customer's phone numbers.

Listing 16.3 – Example of `REPLACE()` function usage.

```sql
SELECT REPLACE(phone, '-', '')
   FROM customers;
```

17. Create a table.

A table is a basic unit which defines how to store data in a relational database. Preparing an SQL script which creates a table verifies if a developer knows how to build a database from scratch and extend an existing one.

CREATE TABLE

You are asked to provide a script which creates a `suppliers` table which contains: identifier, company name, contact data including name, email, and address. The recruiter expects that you can write a script similar to the one presented in Listing 17.1.

Listing 17.1 – Example of `CREATE TABLE` statement usage.

```sql
CREATE TABLE suppliers (
    id int,
    company_name varchar(255),
    contact_name varchar(255),
    address varchar(255),
    country varchar(255),
    email varchar(255)
);
```

CONSTRAINTS

A recruiter also expects that you know that it is possible to put constraints on columns, such as how to prohibit saving `NULL` values, force uniqueness of each value in a column, specify a default value, uniquely identify a row in a table and ensure referential integrity. Listing 17.2 presents an SQL script which contains example constraints.

Listing 17.2 – Example of CREATE TABLE statement with constraints.

```
CREATE TABLE suppliers (
   id int PRIMARY KEY,
   company_name varchar(255) NOT NULL,
   contact_name varchar(255),
   address varchar(255),
   country varchar(255) DEFAULT 'USA',
   email varchar(255) UNIQUE
);
```

18. Modify database schema.

I have worked in the IT industry for many years, and never encountered a project in which I did not have to change the data model. Almost every developer creates update scripts which modify the database schema. Creating new tables, copying data, dropping old tables, adding indexes, are good examples of operations performed by the update scripts. However, this interview task is only about creating a new column, filling it with data, and then dropping the old column.

ALTER TABLE

Developers are usually asked to introduce a new column: `supplier_id` and fill it with data before they remove the `supplier` column from the `products` table. The `products.supplier` and `suppliers.company_name` contain the same text values: the name of the supplier company. In short, the goal of this task is to create a `supplier_id` column which references the `id` column of the `suppliers` table. Listing 18.1 presents an input database schema for this task.

Listing 18.1 – Example database schema.

```
CREATE TABLE suppliers (
    id int PRIMARY KEY,
    company_name varchar(255),
    contact_name varchar(255),
    address varchar(255)
    country varchar(255),
    email varchar(255)
);

CREATE TABLE products (
    id int,
    name varchar(255),
    available bit,
    price decimal(19,2),
    supplier varchar(255)
);
```

Listing 18.2 presents an SQL update script which modifies database schema using the `ALTER TABLE` statement.

Listing 18.2 – Example usage of `ALTER TABLE` statement.

```sql
ALTER TABLE products ADD COLUMN supplier_id int;
ALTER TABLE products ADD FOREIGN KEY(supplier_id) REFERENCES
suppliers(id);

UPDATE products p SET supplier_id=(SELECT id FROM suppliers s
WHERE p.supplier = s.company_name);

ALTER TABLE products DROP COLUMN supplier;
```

Listing 18.3 presents a definition of table `products` after applying the schema modifications.

Listing 18.3 – The `products` table after database schema modification.

```sql
CREATE TABLE products (
    id int,
    name varchar(255),
    available bit,
    price decimal(19,2),
    supplier_id int,
    FOREIGN KEY (supplier_id) REFERENCES suppliers(id)
);
```

19. Reference integrity.

There are two types of constraints which assure the reference integrity: `PRIMARY KEY` and `FOREIGN KEY`. The `PRIMARY KEY` constraint uniquely identifies a record. It is impossible to create more than one `PRIMARY KEY` constraint on a particular table. The `FOREIGN KEY` constraint is used to mark a column as a reference to another table. A column marked as `FOREIGN KEY` must point to another column marked as `PRIMARY KEY`. It is possible to create more than one `FOREIGN KEY` constraint on a particular table.

PRIMARY and FOREIGN KEY

Given two tables, where the first table contains a reference to a second table, you need to put appropriate constraints on columns to assure reference integrity. After that, you need to explain how reference integrity works and what benefits it provides. Listing 19.1 presents two tables: the `suppliers` table in which the `id` column identifies a row, and the `products` table which contains a column `supplier_id` which links the product with the supplier. To assure reference integrity, you need to mark `suppliers.id` column as `PRIMARY KEY` and `products.supplier_id` as the `FOREIGN KEY`.

Listing 19.1 – Example of reference integrity.

```
CREATE TABLE suppliers (
    id int PRIMARY KEY,
    company_name varchar(255),
    contact_name varchar(255),
    address varchar(255),
    country varchar(255),
    email varchar(255),
);

CREATE TABLE products (
    id int,
    name varchar(255),
    available bit,
    price decimal(19,2),
    supplier_id int,
    FOREIGN KEY (supplier_id) REFERENCES suppliers(id)
);
```

In this case, the term reference integrity means that it is impossible to add a product which points to a supplier which does not exist. Also, it is impossible to remove suppliers when there are products linked to them. The database engine does not allow data integrity constraints to be violated in both tables. Recruiters also like to ask developers how to remove a supplier in this case. The correct solution is to remove all products linked with a given supplier before you delete a supplier.

20. Design one-to-many relationship.

Every developer needs to know how to design a one-to-many relationship.

ONE-TO-MANY

You deal with the one-to-many relationship when one customer can place many orders, while one order can be assigned to only one customer. During the job interview, you are usually asked to design a database schema which stores such a relationship. Listing 20.1 presents a script which implements the one-to-many relationship between customers and orders.

Listing 20.1 – Example of one-to-many relationship.

```sql
CREATE TABLE customers (
    id int PRIMARY KEY,
    first_name varchar(255),
    last_name varchar(255),
    email varchar(255),
    phone varchar(255),
    country varchar(255)
);

CREATE TABLE orders (
    id int PRIMARY KEY,
    order_date date,
    shipped_date date,
    customer_id int NOT NULL,
    FOREIGN KEY (customer_id) REFERENCES customers(id)
);
```

To design a one-to-many relationship you need to create an additional column (for instance `customer_id`) on the "many" side which refers to the table that represents "one" side of the relation. Figure 20.1 presents an example where customer 'Bobby Fisher' placed two orders.

customers

ID	FIRST_NAME	LAST_NAME	EMAIL	PHONE	COUNTRY
1	Boris	Spassky	boris@spassky.com	999-888-123	Russia
2	Akiba	Rubinstein	rubi@chess.com	*NULL*	Poland
3	Bobby	Fischer	bobby@fishcher.com	210-6221-9101-22	USA
4	Jose	Capablanca	play@capablanca.com	032-345-567-678	Cuba

orders

ID	ORDER_DATE	SHIPPED_DATE	CUSTOMER_ID
1	2014-11-25	2014-12-02	3
2	2016-12-02	2016-12-09	3
3	2017-02-10	2017-02-18	1
4	2018-03-10	2018-03-19	4
5	2019-09-20	2019-09-30	4

Figure 20.1 – One-to-many relationship represented by database rows.

A recruiter may also ask you: why should you not create a column in `customers` table, named `order_ids` where a list of all identifiers of orders placed is stored as a single value? The correct answer is: such a design can be easily corrupted because it lacks referential integrity. While keeping orders inside the `customers` table is not a bad idea when the system contains a huge amount of data and performance is crucial. However, this topic should be discussed during a NoSQL job interview.

21. Design many-to-many relationship.

Designing the many-to-many relationship using a relational database schema is not obvious. Believe me or not, many developers find challenging to design such a relationship.

MANY-TO-MANY

You are dealing with the many-to-many relationship when a single product can be added to many orders, while one order can store many products. You need to design such a relationship using a well-known "trick". The trick is that you have to create an additional table which stores the many-to-many relation between both sides. Listing 21.1 presents a database schema which represents the many-to-many relationship between orders and products.

Listing 21.1 – Example of many-to-many relationship.

```
CREATE TABLE orders (
    id int PRIMARY KEY,
    order_date date,
    shipped_date date
);

CREATE TABLE products (
    id int PRIMARY KEY,
    name varchar(255),
    available bit,
    price decimal(19,2),
    supplier varchar(255)
);

CREATE TABLE order_items (
    order_id int,
    product_id int,
    quantity int,
    price decimal(19,2),
    discount decimal(19,2),
    PRIMARY KEY (order_id, product_id),
    FOREIGN KEY (order_id) REFERENCES orders(id),
    FOREIGN KEY (product_id) REFERENCES products(id)
);
```

products

ID	NAME	AVAILABLE	PRICE	SUPPLIER
1	Baby diaper	true	12	Brandon
2	Crossland bike	true	780	X-Bikes
3	Bicycle helmet	true	50	X-Bikes
4	Energy drink	false	5	Nutrition-V
5	LED bulb	true	30	Electronics Master

ORDER_ID	PRODUCT_ID	QUANTITY	PRICE	DISCOUNT
1	2	1	780	0
1	3	1	50	0
2	3	2	50	50
3	5	1	30	30

orders

ID	ORDER_DATE	SHIPPED_DATE	CUSTOMER_ID
1	2014-11-25	2014-12-02	3
2	2016-12-02	2016-12-09	3
3	2017-02-10	2017-02-18	1
4	2018-03-10	2018-03-19	4
5	2019-09-20	2019-09-30	4

Figure 21.1 – Many-to-many relationship represented by database rows.

The `order_items` table which is also known as a **join table**, stores a relation between both sides: `orders` and `products`. Figure 21.1 presents an example of the many-to-many relationship, where order with number 1 contains two different products, while the product with identity number 3 (Bicycle helmet) occurs in two different orders.

Recruiters like to ask developers if it is possible to put additional data into the join table. The correct answer is: yes. As presented in Listing 21.1, the join table `order_items` contains additional columns such as `quantity`, `price`, `discount`.

22. Copy data from one table to another table.

A statement which copies specified data from an existing table into a new table is helpful to create a partial backup. Recruiters like to ask about this during a job interview because such a task can be done in various ways. Unfortunately, many developers waste time with the IO operations by exporting data to an external file and then importing it into the new table. Many developers tend to complicate their solutions and dismiss the most simple one.

SELECT INTO

You are asked to create a backup table which contains a copy of all records of the product table. Listing 22.1 presents an example of such a solution.

Listing 22.1 – Example of SELECT INTO statement usage.

```
SELECT * INTO products_backup_2018
  FROM products;
```

23. Combine the results of more than one SELECT statement.

First of all, not every developer is aware that it is possible to combine the results of different SELECT statements. To do that the result-set must contain the same number of columns which have exactly the same types and must be in the same order. If such conditions are met a developer can use the UNION operator to merge the results.

UNION

A recruiter wants to verify if you know how to use the UNION operator. You are asked to combine the names of all suppliers with names of all customers and return them in the single result. Listing 23.1 presents a correct solution for this task.

Listing 23.1 – Example of UNION operator usage.

```
SELECT contact_name FROM suppliers
UNION
SELECT CONCAT(first_name, ' ', last_name) FROM customers;
```

24. Create and execute a stored procedure.

If a developer has solved basic SQL tasks correctly, recruiters like to ask them about more advanced ones, and a stored procedure is one of them. A stored procedure is used to group many SQL queries into a single procedure.

CREATE PROCEDURE

You are asked to create a stored procedure which deletes a supplier from the database, keeping in mind that all products connected with a supplier need to be removed also.

Listing 24.1 – Example of stored procedure definition.

```
CREATE PROCEDURE delete_supplier @supplier_id int AS
BEGIN
   DELETE FROM products WHERE supplier_id = @supplier_id;
   DELETE FROM suppliers WHERE id = @supplier_id;
END;
```

EXEC

Next, you are asked to execute a stored procedure with sample parameters as presented in Listing 24.2.

Listing 24.2 – Execution of stored procedure.

```
EXEC delete_supplier supplier_id = 22;
```

25. Create a view and get data from it.

A developer who is familiar with the concept of database table also needs to be familiar with virtual table (view).

CREATE VIEW

To verify if you understand the idea behind a view, you are asked to create a view which represents all available products without the supplier column. Listing 25.1 presents how to create such a view. Please notice that a view can be a part of SELECT statement in the same way as any other database table.

Listing 25.1 – Example of database view.

```sql
CREATE VIEW available_products AS
  SELECT id, name, price
  FROM products
  WHERE available = TRUE;

SELECT * FROM available_products;
```

26. Create and use a partition.

Nowadays many systems face the problem of increasing amounts of data. A developer needs to be familiar with concepts previously known only to database administrators. In many cases, the only way to speed up the execution of queries performed on large data-sets is to split the data and execute queries on those smaller data-parts.

PARTITION BY

Let us assume that a small e-commerce system grows and suddenly it got new customers from many different countries from all over the world. To speed up queries execution, you need to split data into separate partitions according to the geo-localization of customers. Listing 26.1 presents an example script which creates and uses such partitions.

Listing 26.1 – Example of database partitions defined by list.

```sql
CREATE TABLE customers (
    id int PRIMARY KEY,
    first_name varchar(255),
    last_name varchar(255),
    email varchar(255),
    phone varchar(255),
    country varchar(255)
)
PARTITION BY LIST (country) (
  PARTITION europe VALUES ('Germany', 'Poland', 'England'),
  PARTITION americas VALUES  ('USA', 'Canada'),
  PARTITION africa VALUES ('RPA'),
  PARTITION oceania VALUES ('Australia', 'New Zealand')
);

--use americas partition
SELECT * FROM customers WHERE country = 'USA';

--use europe partition
SELECT * FROM customers WHERE country = 'Poland';
```

Fortunately, the orders table also grows, and it has billions of rows. You are asked to split data in the orders table in following way: all orders before 2015 should be placed in one partition, while other partitions should store orders according to the year when the order was placed. Listing 26.2 presents a correct solution.

Listing 26.2 – Example of database partitions defined by range.

```sql
CREATE TABLE orders (
    id int PRIMARY KEY,
    order_date date,
    shipped_date date,
    customer_id int NOT NULL,
    FOREIGN KEY (customer_id) REFERENCES customers(id)
)
PARTITION BY RANGE(YEAR(order_date)) (
  PARTITION before2016 VALUES LESS THAN (2016),
  PARTITION y2016 VALUES LESS THAN (2017),
  PARTITION y2017 VALUES LESS THAN (2018),
  PARTITION y2018 VALUES LESS THAN (2019),
  PARTITION y2019 VALUES LESS THAN MAXVALUE
);

--use before2016 partition
SELECT * FROM orders WHERE order_date = '2014-09-10';

--use y2018 partition
SELECT * FROM orders WHERE order_date = '2018-06-21';
```

27. Create a query which allows pagination.

To visualize a list of 154 products on a website that was designed to present 20 products at once, a developer has to create queries which provide pagination of results.

PAGINATION

Unfortunately, the SQL standard does not provide keywords such as PAGE SIZE and PAGE NUMBER. Moreover, each database vendor provides a different syntax to implement paging. For example, to select only the specified amount of records, MySQL provides a LIMIT clause, SQL-Server provides TOP keyword while OracleDB supports ROWNUM variable. The goal of this coding task is to check if you can implement paging from any database vendor, which is why a recruiter usually introduces you to available features and then verifies how you use them.

LIMIT

Given the LIMIT clause in the MySQL database, which takes two arguments: offset and number of rows to return, you need to prepare a query which supports pagination of results. The correct solution of this task is to calculate the value of offset based on PAGE NUMBER and PAGE SIZE as presented in Listing 27.1.

Listing 27.1 – Formula for SQL query that supports pagination (MySQL).

```
--@PAGE_SIZE = 20;
--@OFFSET = (@PAGE_NUMBER - 1) * @PAGE_SIZE;

SELECT * FROM available_products LIMIT @OFFSET, @PAGE_SIZE;
```

Listing 27.2 presents example queries which support the pagination of results.

Listing 27.2 – Example queries which get page using LIMIT clause (MySQL).

```
--@PAGE_NUMBER = 1
SELECT * FROM available_products LIMIT 0, 20;

--@PAGE_NUMBER = 2
SELECT * FROM available_products LIMIT 20, 20;

--@PAGE_NUMBER = 3
SELECT * FROM available_products LIMIT 40, 20;
```

OFFSET-FETCH

Given the `OFFSET` clause which defines an offset and the `FETCH NEXT` clause which defines the number of rows to return in SQL Server 2012 database, you need to prepare a query which supports pagination of results. Similar to the MySQL database, the offset must be calculated in the same way as presented in Listing 27.3.

Listing 27.3 – Formula for SQL query that supports pagination (SQL Server 2012).

```
--@PAGE_SIZE = 20;
--@OFFSET = (@PAGE_NUMBER - 1) * @PAGE_SIZE;

SELECT * FROM available_products
ORDER BY id
OFFSET @OFFSET ROWS
FETCH NEXT @PAGE_SIZE ROWS ONLY;
```

Listing 27.4 presents example queries which support the pagination in SQL Server database.

Listing 27.4 – Example queries which get page using OFFSET & FETCH clauses (SQL Server).

```
--@PAGE_NUMBER = 1
SELECT * FROM available_products
ORDER BY id
OFFSET 0 ROWS
FETCH NEXT 20 ROWS ONLY;

--@PAGE_NUMBER = 2
SELECT * FROM available_products
ORDER BY id
OFFSET 20 ROWS
FETCH NEXT 20 ROWS ONLY;
```

```sql
--@PAGE_NUMBER = 3
SELECT * FROM available_products
ORDER BY id
OFFSET 40 ROWS
FETCH NEXT 20 ROWS ONLY;
```

28. Create and use a sequence.

In most scenarios, the unique identifier of a record is generated automatically by a database. When a developer inserts a new row to a table, he does not have to explicitly pass the value of the identifier because the database system increments the identifier by one for each new record. The storage, which keeps the last record ID is also known as a sequence.

SEQUENCE

Despite the `SEQUENCE` and `IDENTITY` keywords are part of SQL standard, each database engine implements a sequence using a different syntax. You are usually asked to create an automatically incremented column in a way chosen by you. Listing 28.1 presents example solutions of how to create and use a sequence in SQL Server, MySQL, and Oracle databases.

Listing 28.1 – Creating a sequence using different databases.

```
--SQLServer: IDENTITY
CREATE TABLE customers (
    id int IDENTITY(1,1) PRIMARY KEY,
    first_name varchar(255),
    last_name varchar(255),
    birth_date date,
    email varchar(255),
    phone varchar(255),
    country varchar(255)
);

--MySQL: AUTO_INCREMENT
CREATE TABLE customers (
    id int NOT NULL AUTO_INCREMENT,
    first_name varchar(255),
    last_name varchar(255),
    birth_date date,
    email varchar(255),
    phone varchar(255),
    country varchar(255)
);
```

```sql
--Oracle: SEQUENCE
CREATE SEQUENCE seq_customer MINVALUE 1
  START WITH 1 INCREMENT BY 1 CACHE 10;

INSERT INTO customers (id, first_name, last_name, birth_date)
  VALUES (seq_customer.nextval, 'Magnus', 'Carlsen', '1990-11-30');
```

29. Create a database trigger.

Another advanced topic likely asked during an SQL coding interview is a trigger. A trigger is a kind of listener which reacts to database-events such as INSERT, UPDATE or DELETE and executes a predefined set of instructions.

CREATE TRIGGER

During a coding interview, a recruiter needs to quickly verify if a developer is familiar with the basic concept. That is why such a coding task is usually not complicated. For example, you are asked to write a trigger which reacts when a new order is added to the database, by adding a log record to the `journal` table indicating the date and time of the event.

Listing 29.1 – Example of a database trigger.

```
CREATE TRIGGER new_order
AFTER INSERT ON orders
FOR EACH ROW
BEGIN
  INSERT INTO journal VALUES ('new_order', NEW.id, CURRENT_TIMESTAMP());
END;
```

30. Define a transaction.

Transactions allow to group related SQL statements and execute them as a single atomic operation. The goal of this SQL coding task is to verify if a developer knows how to declare, execute and undo a transaction.

START TRANSACTION

Although the SQL standard defines the START TRANSACTION statement to begin a transaction, not all database engines follow it, and different keywords are supported such as BEGIN, BEGIN TRANSACTION, or SET TRANSACTION. From the perspective of a recruiter, it does not matter which dialect you use because a recruiter wants to verify if a developer can use the transaction system properly. You are usually asked to perform a couple of operations in the transaction context. For example, new products have been delivered to the shop, and you need to increase the quantity column for many products at once. Please increase the number of all products from 'X-Bikes' supplier by ten, and increase the number of all products from the 'Nutrition-V' supplier by fifty.

Listing 30.1 – Example of a database transaction.

```
START TRANSACTION;

UPDATE products SET amount = amount + 10 WHERE supplier = 'X-Bikes';
UPDATE products SET amount = amount + 50 WHERE supplier = 'Nutrition-V';

COMMIT;

--alternatively undo
ROLLBACK;
```

Contents

www.ingramcontent.com/pod-product-compliance
Lightning Source LLC
Chambersburg PA
CBHW041150050326
40689CB00004B/720